FOOTBALL: RULES OF THE GAME

BRYANT LLOYD

The Rourke Book Co., Inc.
Vero Beach, Florida 32964

EDITORIAL SERVICES:
Penworthy Learning Systems

Library of Congress Cataloging-in-Publication Data

Lloyd, Bryant. 1942
   Football: rules of the game / by Bryant Lloyd.
     p. cm. — (Football)
   Includes index
   Summary: Provides a simple introduction to the game of football, covering layout of the field, rules of play, scoring, and terminology.
   ISBN 1-55916-214-7 (alk. paper)
   1. Football—Rules—Juvenile literature. [1. Football.]
I. Title II. Series
GV955.L56 1997
796.332'02'024—dc21

                                    97–4238
                                         CIP
                                         AC

Printed in the USA

TABLE OF CONTENTS

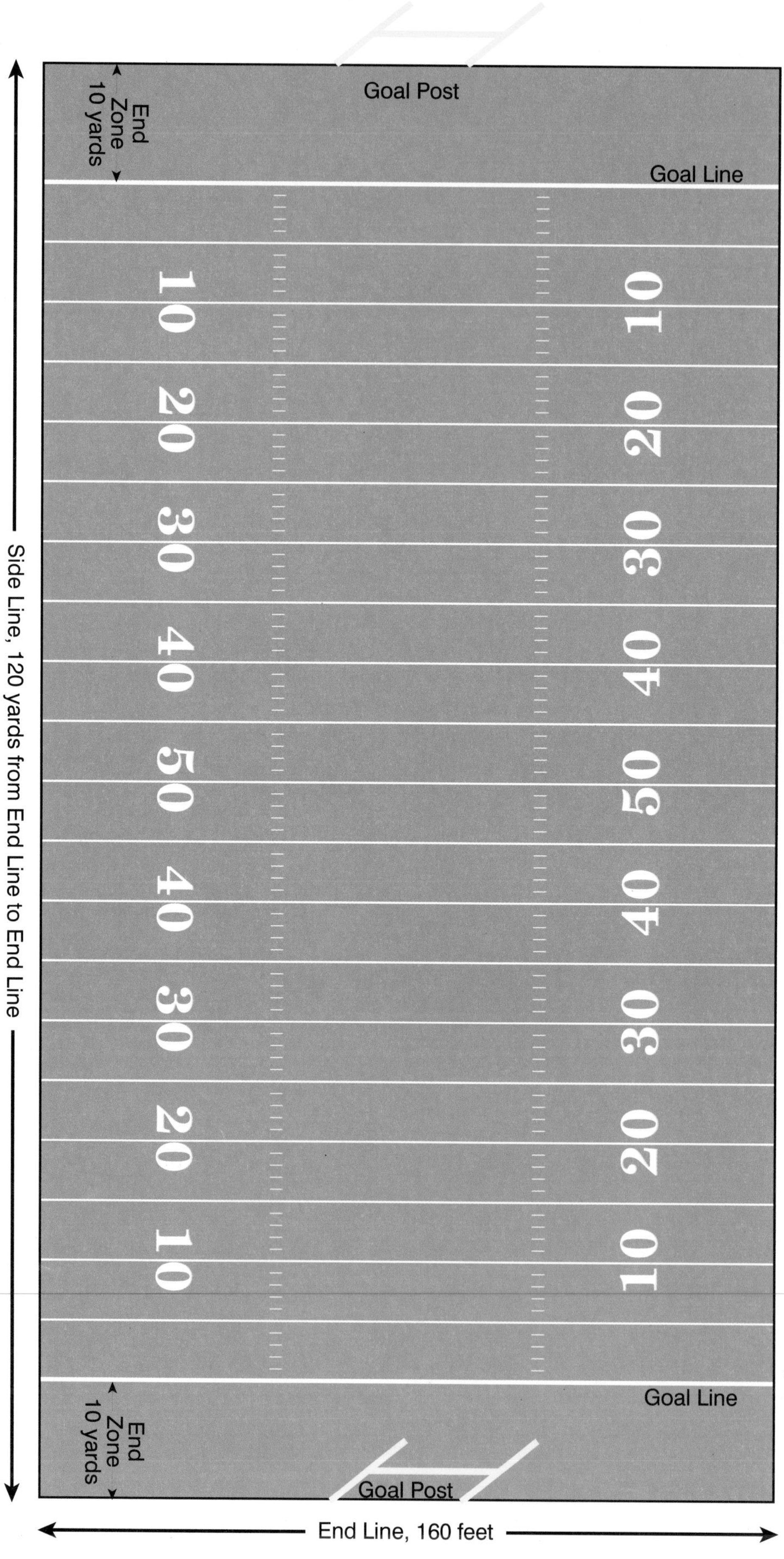

Goal Post

End Zone 10 yards

Goal Line

10

20

30

40

50

40

30

20

10

01

02

03

04

05

04

03

02

01

Side Line, 120 yards from End Line to End Line

100 yards from Goal Line to Goal Line

Goal Line

End Zone 10 yards

Goal Post

End Line, 160 feet

THE FIELD

Football is played on a flat, open field. U.S. fields are 120 yards (110 meters) long from end zone to end zone and 53-1/3 yards (45 meters) wide. Canadian football fields are 160 yards (146 meters) long and 65 yards (59 meters) wide.

Most football fields are outdoors, and they have grass surfaces. Some fields, however, have a **synthetic** (sin THET ik) surface like carpet.

Goal posts rise from each end of a football field. The goal posts are important for scoring points by kicks.

Instant replay is a system that permits football officials to watch a play over and over on tape. After viewing the tape, officials can decide how to rule on a play.

Diagram shows dimensions of American football field.

FIELD STRIPES

Football fields are marked with white stripes. They show boundaries and distances. Yard lines cross the field every 10 yards (9 meters).

Each team defends a goal line. The two goal lines are 100 yards (91 meters) apart on an American field and 110 yards (just over 100 meters) apart on Canadian fields.

Yard lines (white stripes across field), side lines (white stripe from left to right in photo), and yard markers (10) mark a football field.

Line of scrimmage is an imaginary line. It falls wherever the football is placed by the official. Players line up on each side of this line, but not on it.

End lines and side lines around the field mark the area of play. Players who cross the side lines or end lines are out of bounds.

Hash marks are short stripes placed one yard (almost one meter) apart.

STARTING A GAME

A football game begins with two teams on the field. Each team has 11 players (12 in Canada).

One team kicks the football to the other. It is called the kickoff. The team that receives the kick becomes the **offense** (AW fents). The kick receiver runs forward, toward the kicking team's goal. He runs until he is tackled or steps out of bounds.

Wherever he is tackled becomes the **line of scrimmage** (LYN UV SKRIM idj). That is the starting point for the offensive team's first play.

Football game begins with the kickoff. One team kicks to another. The receiving team puts the football into play.

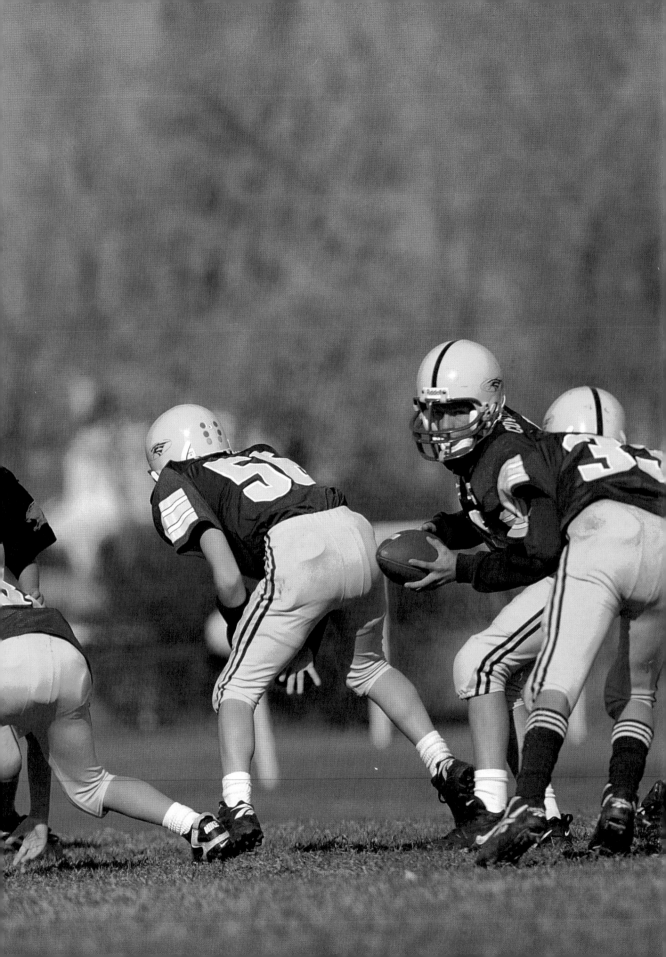

MOVING THE BALL

With each play, the offense tries to advance the ball toward the **defense's** (DEE fents ez) goal line. A team advances most often by handing or throwing the football to a ball carrier. When he is tackled to the ground or steps out of bounds, the play ends. If the ball carrier scores a touchdown by crossing the goal line of the defense, his team kicks off to that team.

The offense has four **downs** (DOUNZ), or plays, to advance the ball 10 yards (9 meters) from its original line of scrimmage. If the offense makes 10 yards (9 meters), it is given a new set of four downs.

A sweep is a running play in which the ball carrier runs around the end of the line. With an option play, the ball carrier may choose to pass or run.

The ball has been snapped from the center to the quarterback. The offense is now running its play from the line of scrimmage.

DOWNS

Each set of downs begins with a first down. If a team does not make 10 yards (9 meters) in its first three downs, it may punt. To punt, the punter kicks the football to the other team. A team usually punts on its fourth down.

This team is attempting to move the ball forward and gain yards by running.

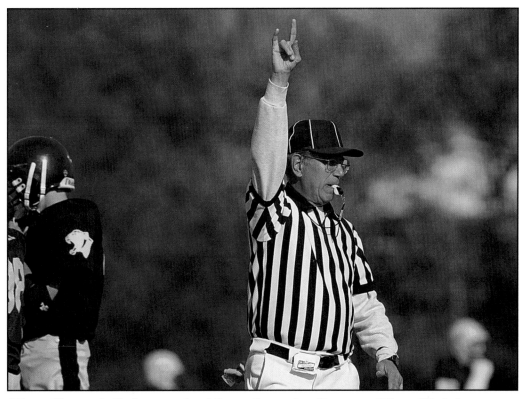

The offense failed to make 10 yards on its first try. The official now signals second down.

A team does not have to punt, though. It can use the fourth down to advance the ball. What happens if it fails to make 10 yards (9 meters)? It must give up the ball where it lies after the fourth-down play.

LOSING THE BALL

An offensive team can also lose the ball on interceptions and lost fumbles. An interception is a thrown ball that is caught by a defensive player.

Only certain offensive players can pass, or throw, the football forward, and only to certain teammates. A pass can be intercepted, or caught, by anyone on the defensive team.

A fumble is a ball muffed, or dropped, by the ball carrier. A fumble can be seized by any player of either team.

Clipping is a kind of illegal block. An offensive player clips if he blocks a defensive player from behind beyond the line of scrimmage.

The ball carrier (white jersey, 5) fumbled. Now a player from either team can pounce on the ball.

TOUCHDOWNS

The biggest football score, worth 6 points, is a touchdown, or TD. After a touchdown, the scoring team tries a **conversion** (kun VER zhun), or extra point. A short place kick over the crossbar and between the goal posts counts one point.

The scoring team may also choose to try a two-point conversion. It can be a short run or a completed pass over the goal line.

Colleges and high schools begin their conversion attempts from the three-yard (almost 3 meters) line. The National Football League (NFL) begins at the two-yard (almost 2 meters) line.

Just a step from the goal line, the ball carrier rushes toward a touchdown.

OTHER SCORES

A safety is another type of two-point score. A safety occurs when a ball carrier is tackled in his own end zone. The end zone is the area 10 yards (9 meters) behind the goal line in American football.

Running back dashes into the end zone for a two-point conversion after his team's touchdown.

By tackling a ball carrier in his team's end zone, a defense earns a safety—and two points.

A field goal kick is worth three points. Like an extra point, a field goal kick must clear the crossbar and stay within the goal posts. A field goal, though, may be tried from wherever the offense has the football.

OFFICIALS

Football **officials** (uh FISH ulz) direct the play of the game. One official keeps the clock. Football games are played for a fixed number of minutes. Colleges and NFL teams play four 15-minute quarters. High schools play 12-minute quarters. The game clock is stopped after incomplete passes and for several other reasons.

Other officials whistle the end of play. They also watch for plays that break football rules. They signal a **penalty** (PEN ul tee) if they see a rule broken. A penalty results in the loss of yards or downs.

Football officials carry "flags" as well as whistles. Their flags are yellow cloth. When an official sees an illegal play, he throws the flag.

Officials keep the time clock, call penalties, and direct the play of a football game.